Diabetic Recipes
Healthy and Delicious Low-Carb Recipes to Lower Blood Sugar

Savannah Gibbs

© **Text Copyright 2018 by Savannah Gibbs - All rights reserved.**

This document is geared towards providing exact and reliable information in regards to the topic and issue covered. The publication is sold with the idea that the publisher is not required to render accounting, officially permitted, or otherwise, qualified services. If advice is necessary, legal or professional, a practiced individual in the profession should be ordered.

From a Declaration of Principles which was accepted and approved equally by a Committee of the American Bar Association and a Committee of Publishers and Associations.

In no way is it legal to reproduce, duplicate, or transmit any part of this document in either electronic means or in printed format. Recording of this publication is strictly prohibited and any storage of this document is not allowed unless with written permission from the publisher. All rights reserved.

The information provided herein is stated to be truthful and consistent, in that any liability, in terms of inattention or otherwise, by any usage or abuse of any policies, processes, or directions contained within is the solitary and utter responsibility of the recipient reader. Under no circumstances will any legal responsibility or blame be held against the publisher for any reparation, damages, or monetary loss due to the information herein, either directly or indirectly.

Respective authors own all copyrights not held by the publisher.

The information herein is offered for informational purposes solely, and is universal as so. The presentation of the information is without contract or any type of guarantee assurance.

The trademarks that are used are without any consent, and the publication of the trademark is without permission or backing by the trademark owner. All trademarks and brands within this book are for clarifying purposes only and are owned by the owners themselves, not affiliated with this document.

Table of Contents

Introduction 1

Chapter 1: What is a Diabetes Diet? 3

    Why Should You Limit Your Carbohydrate Intake? 4
    Why You Should Avoid Sugar 5
    Why Fruits and Vegetables are Good for Diabetics 6
    Diabetes Superfoods 6
    Why You Should Choose the Type of Fat You Eat 7
    Why Cut Back on Sodium? 8
    Additional Things You Can Do 8

Chapter 2: Diabetic Breakfast Recipes 10

    Spinach and Onion Scramble 10
    Carrot Bread 12
    Baked Granola with Fruit 14
    Banana Coconut Smoothie 15
    Scrambled Eggs with Mushroom and Spinach 16
    Tomato and Zucchini Omelet 17
    Easy Spanish Eggs 19
    Baked Eggs with Kidney Beans 20
    Banana and Peanut Butter Drop Scones 21
    Asparagus and Ham Egg Muffins 23
    Berry Porridge 24
    Avocado Toast with Mexican Salsa 25
    Blueberry Mini Pancakes 26
    Cherry Coconut Oatmeal 28

Chapter 3: Diabetic Lunch Recipes 30

    Roasted Celery Root with Baby Carrots 30
    Green Olive and Pork Quesadillas 32
    Spinach Salad with Shrimp 34

Turkey and Spinach Salad 35
Green Bean and Anchovy Salad 36
Spicy Tomato Couscous 37
Easy Chicken Taco Pizzas 39
Rosemary Chicken Wrap 40
Breadless Bruschetta 41
Quinoa and Black Beans 42
Fish and Squash Meal 43
Grilled Vegetables 45

Chapter 4: Diabetic Friendly Snacks 47

Tuna on Cukes 48
Roasted Seeds and Nuts 49
Stuffed Mushrooms 50
Celery Zucchini Smoothie 51
Bitter Berry Smoothie 52
Apple Pie Smoothie 53
Sweet Potato Fries 54
Carrot Cake Cookies 55
Oven Baked Grapefruit 57
Edamame and Guacamole 58
Spicy Popcorn 59
Pumpkin Bars 60

Chapter 5: Diabetic Dinner Recipes 62

Rosemary Chicken and Rice 62
Spicy Chicken Stew 64
Chicken with Parmesan Crust 66
Ginger Steak 67
Sautéed Spicy Shrimp 68
Bitter Melon Curry 69
Meatballs Curry 71
Chili Beef Pasta 73
Spicy Lamb with Peas 74
Spicy Turkey and Beans 76

vii

Thai Turkey Paleo Mix 77
Turkey with Lentils and Veggies 79
Cheesy Spinach Bake 81
Twice-Baked Squash 83
Herb Crusted Salmon with Spinach 84
Salmon and Asparagus 86
Roasted Mackerel 87
Tomato & Vegetable Quinoa Pilaf 88

Conclusion 90
Check Out My Other Books 92

Introduction

Diabetes is a leading cause of death in the United States, affecting more than 29 million people. It is rightly being called an epidemic, since there are so many people who are affected. The disease itself is not fatal and with the right medication and lifestyle, diabetics can avoid dangerous complications caused by uncontrolled blood glucose and live a long, active, and fruitful life.

Unlike what many people might think, food does not cause diabetes, but when you're already a diabetic, your choice of food matters. This is why doctors and dietitians will recommend that you go on a diabetes diet.

Does this mean you can only eat bland and tasteless food? No, but it does mean you need to know which foods will help you maintain your blood sugar and which ones will cause it to spike.

I know you hate feeling deprived of the food you love to eat, which is why I've written this book for you, containing healthy and delicious recipes recommended for diabetics. Whoever said diabetic food can't be both?

You can cook these breakfast, lunch, snack, and dinner recipes while familiarizing yourself with the types of food that are good for you and which of the food groups you need to avoid. Coupled with medication and regular exercise, eating right can help to manage your blood glucose, and in some people, it has even reversed their diabetes, allowing them to control their blood sugar levels without medication. Wouldn't it be wonderful if that happens?

I hope you enjoy these recipes. After tasting these delicious fares you'll realize that eating right doesn't have to mean depriving yourself of the foods you enjoy. You only need to find healthier alternatives and be creative.

Bon appetit!

Chapter 1: What is a Diabetes Diet?

Once you're a diabetic, your choice of food will directly affect the results of your diabetes management program, which involves the following:
- taking the right medication regularly;
- monitoring blood glucose levels;
- having an active lifestyle; and
- going on a diabetes diet.

Of all of the above, the mention of a diabetes diet instantly elicits a negative response from diabetics who already may feel deprived and depressed. This is understandable, since food is a source of comfort and gratification for us humans. Not only do we need to eat, but we love to eat.

Is going on a diabetes diet as bad as it sounds? What does that mean anyway?

A diabetes diet is not a condemnation to a lifetime of bland and tasteless food—it simply means eating foods that are low in carbohydrates and added sugar, low in fat, low in sodium, high in nutrition, high in protein, and moderate to low in calories.

What do you think? Are you still thinking that means a piece of cardboard served on a plate? That's the usual reaction. At the mention of all of these "lows," diabetics fear they may never enjoy food again. It's a sad thought, but one that is totally baseless. Before I tell you why you don't need to be sad and feel deprived, I'd like to share with you the WHY of the diabetes diet. Why do you need to lower your intake of sugar, carbohydrates, salt, and fats? Why do you need to lose weight? Once you know why you need to watch what you eat and drink, you will be more motivated and have the determination to stick to your program.

Why Should You Limit Your Carbohydrate Intake?

Diabetes is a disease in which the body is unable to properly process carbohydrates. Insulin, which is produced by the pancreas, is responsible for breaking down carbohydrate intakes by enabling cells to absorb blood sugar. Diabetics either don't produce enough insulin, or their cells do not respond to insulin like they should. The result is that blood sugar levels reach abnormal levels and the sugar molecules are left to circulate in the bloodstream, causing tissue damage, which is not a good thing.

To avoid this from happening, you should limit carbohydrate intake when you can. Carbs become sugar and sugar must be avoided as much as possible. The best way to keep your sugar levels low is to prevent them from spiking in the first place.

Since we need carbohydrates for energy, it is not advised that you remove them from your diet entirely. A balanced diet is still preferable to ensure you're getting all of the sustenance you need.

Diabetics should aim for 45 to 60 grams of carbohydrates per meal and 15 to 30 grams for snacks. Choose complex carbohydrates found in beans, whole grains, and vegetables instead of simple carbohydrates, such as sugar and corn syrup. Since people respond to carbohydrates differently, the best way to know if you are getting too much is to test yourself after each meal. Count the carbs in your food to see how much it affects your blood sugar levels. To further integrate carbohydrate monitoring into your diabetes treatment, a dietitian can help set specific goals for carbohydrates to be included in each meal and snack.

Why You Should Avoid Sugar

If a diabetic is advised to limit carbohydrates because they turn to sugar, it follows that sugar itself should be avoided. Sodas, candies, sports drinks, fruit drinks—all of these beverages will catapult your sugar levels to unwanted heights, not to mention that they contain a lot of calories.

To give you an example: one can of regular soda contains around 10 teaspoons of sugar and 150 calories. When you think about how much soda a regular person consumes in one sitting, it's no wonder we've become sugar addicts.

The World Health Organization initially set the recommended daily intake of sugar to 10% of your total calories—that's 200 calories. In their latest recommendation, they've lowered it further to just 5%, equivalent to 100 calories. As one teaspoon of sugar is 16 calories, you are technically only allowed six teaspoons of sugar a day, way less than what we're used to consuming.

Not only does sugar raise your blood glucose levels, it can also cause fatty liver, which is common among diabetics. In a recent study by the US Centers for Disease Control and Prevention, it was concluded that large amounts of additional sugar in a diet increases the risk of heart disease by as much as 30%.

Sugar is hard to avoid because not only is it delicious, but most food labels hide the sugar content. Anything that ends in "ose" is sugar-related, including high-fructose corn syrup (HFCS), caramel, treacle, malt syrup, maltodextrin, fruit concentrate, and more. The good news is that there are many sugar-free alternatives available nowadays.

Why Fruits and Vegetables are Good for Diabetics

For people dealing with diabetes, a plant-based diet is the best option for their health. This means filling your plate with fruits and vegetables. The reason fruits and vegetables work so well for the diabetes diet is that they are packed with vitamins, minerals, and other nutrients. They are low in fat and calories, and the fiber they contain helps slow down the absorption of glucose in the body.

Five portions—roughly what will fit in your palm—is the recommended amount of daily fruits and vegetables.

Large, healthy salads are always a good choice. Add flavor by topping salads with protein like chicken, tuna, or shrimp. Sprinkle it with nuts and seeds and enjoy a homemade dressing made with olive oil, vinegar, and your favorite spices. Fruit makes an excellent snack when you're craving something sweet, especially berries, apples, and cantaloupe.

When you're planning meals or looking for a snack, make sure that at least half of your plate is covered with a combination of fruits and vegetables. Combined with whole grains and low-fat protein sources, you'll create a healthy, balanced diet that allows you to lower your blood sugar, protect your heart, and feel a lot better.

Diabetes Superfoods

Studies have shown that some vegetables and spices are especially helpful in lowering blood sugar. These diabetes superfoods include celery, bitter melon, pumpkin, tomatoes, spinach, beans, berries, nuts, and cinnamon. These superfoods can improve the body's sensitivity to insulin, repair damaged cells in the pancreas, and reduce blood sugar levels.

Why You Should Choose the Type of Fat You Eat

Not all fats are created equal; there are good fats and bad fats. This is important to note since diabetics have an increased risk of heart disease and stroke. Watching the type of fats you consume will be a regular part of your diabetes diet.

The bad fats are trans fat and saturated fat which are bad for the heart. Among all of the fats, trans fats are the worst for your health because they increase levels of LDL (bad cholesterol) while reducing levels of HDL (good cholesterol). Trans fats stimulate plaque formation and the clogging of arteries.

Most trans fats that we encounter are produced artificially by the food industry, which hydrogenates vegetable oils to increase shelf life and enhance the flavor of processed foods. Trans fats are by-products of the oil hydrogenation process. Although many fast food restaurants—such as McDonald's, Burger King, and Wendy's—have stopped using hydrogenated vegetable oils to fry food, fried foods from some other restaurants may still contain trans fats. Today, we can still find trans fats in processed foods, cookies, baked goods, cream pies, margarine sticks, and shortening. When shopping for groceries, double-check the trans fat section on Nutrition Facts labels and avoid foods containing "partially hydrogenated" or "hydrogenated vegetable oils."

Good fats include mono-unsaturated or poly-unsaturated fats, found in salmon, flaxseeds, avocado, olive oils, and most nuts.

Why Cut Back on Sodium?

A high-sodium diet also causes high-blood pressure. Similar to the reason why you should cut down on fats, you should also reduce the salt in your food. Diabetics should aim for only 2300 mg of sodium or less daily. Studies have shown that approximately 75% of the sodium in an average American's diet comes from processed and packaged foods.

Eating fresh and unprocessed foods is the easiest way to ensure your sodium intake meets the daily allowance, without putting yourself at a higher risk for heart attack or stroke.

Additional Things You Can Do

In addition to the diabetes diet, there are other things you can do to make your eating plan more successful and keep your diabetes under control. Incorporate exercise into your day as often as possible. If you like being around other people, join a gym or take an exercise class. If you'd rather exercise on your own, simply taking a long walk every day is enough to make a positive difference. Take the stairs when you can instead of the elevator, and park far away from the store when you're shopping instead of cruising for the closest spot. Physical activity in any form will make a difference in how you fight diabetes.

You will also want to get enough rest and learn how to manage your stress. Create healthy routines in your life that will make it easy for you to focus on eating well and taking control of your diabetes. Stress will only make the condition worse, and it's not good for your heart or your blood pressure either. Get support from family and friends, as well as from others who are fighting the same battle as you. There are support groups for diabetics and tons of resources to help you learn how to cook good food and order healthy options in restaurants.

The 56 healthy and delicious recipes in this book are diabetic-friendly. You can cook these breakfast, lunch, snack, and dinner recipes while familiarizing yourself with the diabetes diet.

Chapter 2: Diabetic Breakfast Recipes

Breakfast is a meal that diabetics shouldn't skip, as many diabetics have reported that skipping breakfast makes their blood sugar levels less manageable during the day. Here are some dishes that are easy to prepare to can get your day started right.

Spinach and Onion Scramble

Yield: 4 servings
Ingredients:
6 eggs
1 tablespoon almond milk
6 ounces fresh baby spinach
1 cup red onion, chopped
2 garlic cloves, minced
1 tablespoon olive oil
Salt and pepper to taste

Directions:
1. Heat the olive oil in a skillet over medium heat. Add the garlic and onion, and cook for 3 minutes.
2. Add the spinach and heat until it begins to wilt.
3. While the vegetables are cooking, beat the eggs and the almond milk together.
4. Add the egg mixture to the pan and scramble all ingredients together until the eggs are cooked.
5. Serve with salt and pepper.

Nutritional Information (Per Serving)
Calories: 157
Fat: 11.2 g
Sat Fat: 3.4 g

Carbohydrates: 5.5 g
Fiber: 1.7 g
Sugar: 2.1 g
Protein: 10 g

Carrot Bread

Yield: 8 servings

Ingredients:
2 cups almond flour
1 teaspoon baking powder
1 tablespoon cumin seeds
Salt to taste
3 large eggs
2 tablespoons olive oil
1 tablespoon apple cider vinegar
3 cups carrots, peeled and grated
½ teaspoon fresh ginger, peeled and grated finely
¼ cup raisins

Directions:
1. Preheat your oven to 350 degrees F.
2. Line a loaf pan with parchment paper.
3. In a large bowl, add almond flour, baking powder, cumin seeds, and salt and mix well.
4. In another bowl, add the eggs, olive oil, and vinegar, and beat until well combined.
5. Add egg mixture to the flour mixture, and mix until well combined.
6. Gently fold in carrot, ginger, and raisins.
7. Place the mixture into the prepared loaf pan.
8. Bake for about 1 hour until a toothpick inserted in the center comes out clean.

Nutritional Information (Per Serving)
Calories: 255
Fat: 19.4 g
Sat Fat: 2.1 g
Carbohydrates: 15.3 g
Fiber: 4.6 g
Sugar: 6.4 g

Protein: 9.1 g

Baked Granola with Fruit

Yield: 16 servings
Ingredients:
2 cups steel cut oats
1 cup sunflower seeds
1 cup pumpkin seeds
1 cup raisins
½ cup dried cherries
6 tablespoons coconut oil
1 cup almond flour
2 tablespoons ground ginger
2 tablespoons cinnamon
1 tablespoon allspice
1 tablespoon nutmeg
4 cups almond milk
1 cup fresh blueberries
1 cup fresh strawberries

Directions:
1. Preheat the oven to 350 degrees F.
2. In a large bowl, combine the oats, seeds, raisins, cherries, almond flower, and spices. Mix everything well.
3. Warm the coconut oil until it is in liquid form, and add to the mixture.
4. Pour everything into a baking dish and cook for 20 minutes.
5. Remove the granola from the oven, and allow it to cool.
6. Break up the granola so it's loose and pour it into separate bowls.
7. Add almond milk and sprinkle with berries.
8. You can keep the granola in an airtight container for up to a month.

Nutritional Information (Per Serving)

Calories: 342
Fat: 26.7 g
Sat Fat: 18.3 g
Carbohydrates: 24.6 g
Fiber: 4.9 g
Sugar: 9.7 g
Protein: 6.4 g
Sodium: 14 mg

Banana Coconut Smoothie

Yield: 2 servings
Ingredients:
½ banana, frozen and chopped
2 tablespoons hemp seeds
2 teaspoons lime juice
¼ teaspoon vanilla extract
1 tablespoon unsweetened coconut flakes
1½ cups unsweetened coconut water
Ice

Directions:
1. Blend all ingredients until smooth.

Nutritional Information (Per Serving)
Calories: 194
Fat: 11.3 g
Sat Fat: 4.2 g
Carbohydrates: 16.9 g
Fiber: 4.3 g
Sugar: 9.1 g
Protein: 7.2 g
Sodium: 192 mg

Scrambled Eggs with Mushroom and Spinach

Yield: 2 servings

Ingredients:

2 eggs, large
2 egg whites
1/8 teaspoon salt
1/8 teaspoon pepper
1 teaspoon butter
1/2 cup fresh mushrooms, sliced thin
1/2 cup fresh baby spinach (or your favorite green veggie), chopped
2 tablespoons shredded parmesan cheese

Directions:

1. Beat eggs, egg whites, pepper, and salt in a bowl until thoroughly mixed.
2. Using a small, nonstick skillet, heat the butter over low-medium heat. Cook the mushrooms, stirring as you cook for 3–4 minutes or until tender.
3. Add spinach. Cook until slightly wilted. Lower heat.
4. Add beaten egg mixture and stir until eggs are thickened and thoroughly cooked. Stir in cheese.

Nutritional Information (Per Serving)
Calories: 134
Fat: 8.5 g
Sat Fat: 3.8 g
Carbohydrates: 1.8 g
Fiber: 0.4 g
Sugar: 1 g
Protein: 12.9 g
Sodium: 336 mg

Tomato and Zucchini Omelet

Yield: 4 servings

Ingredients:
1/3 cup sun-dried tomatoes
1 1/2 cups egg substitute
1/2 cup cottage cheese
2 green onions, chopped
1/4 cup minced fresh basil or 1 tablespoon dried basil
1/8 teaspoon crushed red pepper flakes
1 cup fresh broccoli
1 cup zucchini, sliced
1 medium red pepper, chopped
2 teaspoons canola oil
1 cup boiling water
2 tablespoons Parmesan cheese, grated

Directions:

1. Place the tomatoes in a bowl and cover with boiling water. Let stand for 5 minutes. Drain and put aside.

2. In another bowl, mix the egg substitute, onions, basil, pepper flakes, cottage cheese, and tomatoes. Set aside.

3. In a 10-inch oven-proof skillet, sauté the zucchini, red pepper, and broccoli in oil until tender. Lower heat and top with the egg mixture. Cover and cook for 4–6 minutes or until nearly set.

4. Sprinkle with Parmesan cheese, then heat for 2 minutes or until eggs are completely set. Let sit for 5 minutes. Cut into wedges and serve.

Nutritional Information (Per Serving)
Calories: 135
Fat: 3.9 g
Sat Fat: 1 g
Carbohydrates: 7.6 g

Fiber: 1.7 g
Sugar: 3.6 g
Protein: 17.9 g
Sodium: 342 mg

Easy Spanish Eggs

Yield: 4 servings
Ingredients:
7 large eggs
¾ cup low-fat or non-fat milk
1 cup chopped spinach leaves
8 cherry tomatoes, halved
4 multigrain English muffins, halved
½ cup low-fat cheddar cheese, grated
Pepper to taste

Directions:
1. In a large, microwavable dish, whisk the eggs and milk. Microwave for 4 minutes on high.
2. Remove the dish and gently stir. Add the cherry tomatoes, spinach, and cheese and microwave for 2 minutes.
3. Toast the halved muffins and top with the scrambled eggs.
4. Sprinkle with pepper and serve.

Nutritional Information (Per Serving)
Calories: 358
Fat: 14.9 g
Sat Fat: 6.2 g
Carbohydrates: 35.9 g
Fiber: 5.1 g
Sugar: 9.3 g
Protein: 22.2 g
Sodium: 555 mg

Baked Eggs with Kidney Beans

Yield: 4 servings

Ingredients:
1 teaspoon olive oil
2 cloves minced garlic
1 onion, sliced thinly
5 cups baby spinach
2 ½ cups fresh tomatoes, chopped
4 eggs
½ cup canned red kidney beans, rinsed
8 pieces of toasted whole-wheat bread

Directions:
1. Preheat oven to 350 degrees F.
2. In a saucepan, add olive oil and sauté the onion and garlic. Stir for a minute or two until onion is cooked. Add the spinach, then add tomatoes and kidney beans.
3. Allow to simmer and cook covered for five minutes.
4. Grease 4 ramekins with some cooking spray. Divide the tomato mixture among them.
5. Break 1 egg into each ramekin.
6. Place the ramekins on a baking tray. Bake in the oven for 16–18 minutes or until the eggs are set.
7. Remove from the oven and serve with toasts.

Nutritional Information (Per Serving)
Calories: 331
Fat: 8.1 g
Sat Fat: 2 g
Carbohydrates: 46.4 g
Fiber: 10.1 g
Sugar: 8.3 g
Protein: 20.4 g
Sodium: 365 mg

Banana and Peanut Butter Drop Scones

Makes 15 scones

Ingredients:
2 fresh bananas, sliced
1 cup flour
½ teaspoon baking soda
pinch of salt
Stevia to sweeten
1 egg, large
1 apple, cored and finely chopped
1¼ cups non-fat milk
Olive oil, spray
Peanut butter, all natural

Directions:
1. Heat a non-stick skillet over medium-high heat.
2. In a large mixing bowl, sift the flour, salt, baking soda, and Stevia. Make hole in the center of sifted ingredients.
3. Lightly beat the eggs and add milk. Add milk mixture to flour mixture in increments to form a smooth, thick batter. Add banana slices and make sure they're evenly distributed on the batter.
4. Coat a skillet with cooking spray and apply low heat. To make a scone, drop a large tablespoon of batter into hot oil. When bubbles form on top of scone, gently turn and cook about 1 minute until the scone is golden brown.
5. Once cooked, remove scone and keep warm under a clean cloth.
6. Cook the rest of the scones in the same way. Once all of the scones have been cooked, place on a plate and spread peanut butter on top.

Nutritional Information (Per Scone)
Calories: 73

Fat: 0.5 g
Sat Fat: 0.1 g
Carbohydrates: 14.2 g
Fiber: 1 g
Sugar: 5.7 g
Protein: 2.9 g
Sodium: 81 mg

Asparagus and Ham Egg Muffins

Yield: 2 servings

Ingredients:

10 medium spears of asparagus
2 tablespoons apple cider vinegar
2 eggs, large
2 English muffins
2 teaspoons cream cheese, low-fat
1 ounce ham, thinly sliced
Salt and pepper to taste

Directions:

1. Add vinegar to a pan of boiling water. Add asparagus and cook for 5 minutes or until tender.

2. Crack eggs into a separate pan of boiling water and poach for 3 minutes.

3. Cut English muffins in half and toast under a preheated grill. Spread some cream cheese on top.

4. Slice English muffins in half again. Arrange on two plates and top each slice with asparagus and ham.

5. Lastly, top each muffin with a poached egg. Season as desired and serve hot.

Nutritional Information (Per Serving)
Calories: 330
Fat: 7.7 g
Sat Fat: 2.9 g
Carbohydrates: 41.3 g
Fiber: 7.2 g
Sugar: 7.4 g
Protein: 23.2 g

Berry Porridge

Yield: 2 servings
Ingredients:
½ cup rolled oats
6 strawberries, sliced
½ cup raspberries
1 cup blueberries
½ cup non-fat milk
2 teaspoons toasted almonds
1 cup water

Directions:
1. In a pan, add the water and oats. Bring to a boil, then turn heat down and stir for 4 minutes.
2. Add ¾ of the fruit and then add milk. Increase heat, simmer for 1 minute and mix well. Put into a bowl.
3. Put the rest of the fruit and the almonds on top. Serve hot.

Nutritional Information (Per Serving)
Calories: 180
Fat: 2.9 g
Sat Fat: 0.3 g
Carbohydrates: 34.2 g
Fiber: 6.8 g
Sugar: 13.6 g
Protein: 6.3 g
Sodium: 35 mg

Avocado Toast with Mexican Salsa

Yield: 1 serving
Ingredients:
2 slices whole-wheat bread
Half avocado, meat only
¼ cup fresh coriander, roughly chopped
1 ripe tomato, diced
1 tablespoon lemon juice
½ teaspoon black pepper, freshly ground

Directions:
1. Salsa: In a bowl, combine the coriander, lemon juice, diced tomatoes, and black pepper.
2. Preparing the toast: Toast the bread. Spread the avocado evenly onto the bread. Spoon salsa on top.
3. Season to taste.

Nutritional Information (Per Serving)
Calories: 301
Fat: 15.5 g
Sat Fat: 2.4 g
Carbohydrates: 34.2 g
Fiber: 10.9 g
Sugar: 5.4 g
Protein: 9.8 g
Sodium: 280 mg

Blueberry Mini Pancakes

Makes 10 pancakes
Ingredients:
1½ cups flour
1 teaspoon baking powder
1 medium egg, beaten
250 ml non-fat milk
1 teaspoon vanilla extract
1½ cups fresh blueberries
2 teaspoons sunflower oil
1 teaspoon Stevia (optional)

Directions:
1. Combine flour and baking powder in a bowl.
2. Beat the egg in a separate bowl, and add the milk and vanilla extract.
3. Make a pit in the middle of the flour mixture. Add the egg and milk mixture. Stir until batter is smooth. Allow the batter to stand for a few minutes.
4. Crush half of the blueberries with fork and mix into the batter. Add whole blueberries. Make sure they're evenly distributed.
5. Put a small amount of oil in a non-stick pan. Spoon the batter into pan.
6. Cook pancakes on low heat for 2–3 minutes or until you see bubbles form on top. Turn and cook for another 2 minutes.
7. Sprinkle with a little Stevia before serving, if you prefer. You can also use sugar-free pancake syrup or spoon on some low-fat yogurt.

Nutritional Information (Per Pancake)
Calories: 140
Fat: 1.8 g

Sat Fat: 0.3 g
Carbohydrates: 27.4 g
Fiber: 2.5 g
Sugar: 9.3 g
Protein: 4 g
Sodium: 21 mg

Cherry Coconut Oatmeal

Yield: 6 servings
Ingredients:
1 cup steel cut oats
3 cups coconut milk
1 cup fresh cherries, chopped
2 tablespoons raw honey
¼ cup dark chocolate, shaved

Directions:
1. Cook oats in the coconut milk, simmering until all the liquid is absorbed.
2. Stir in the cherries and add the honey.
3. Serve in bowls and top with dark chocolate shavings.

Nutritional Information (Per Serving)
Calories: 399
Fat: 31.7 g
Sat Fat: 27 g
Carbohydrates: 29 g
Fiber: 4.7 g
Sugar: 15.7 g
Protein: 5.4 g
Sodium: 25 mg

Breakfast is the most important meal of the day, as everyone knows. With these diabetic breakfast recipes, you'll give yourself a fighting chance to manage your diabetes and stay on a healthy course for the remainder of the day.

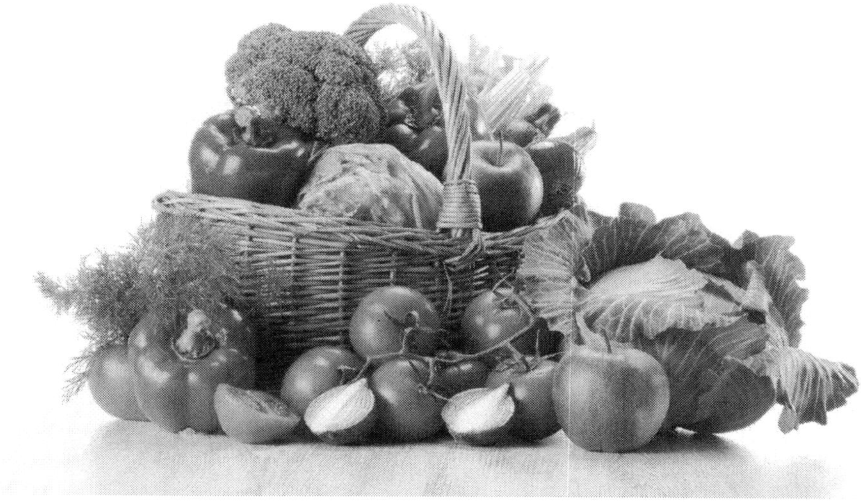

Chapter 3: Diabetic Lunch Recipes

For diabetics, healthy and nutritious food can be mouth-watering, too. These delicious lunch recipes are perfectly suited to give you the energy you need for the day. They are low fat, low carb, and most are high in fiber. Try some of them, then experiment with your own.

Roasted Celery Root with Baby Carrots

Yield: 4 servings
Ingredients:
1 pound celery root, diced into 1-inch squares
2 teaspoons olive oil
1 small pinch of black pepper
2 inch-long sprigs of fresh rosemary
½ pound baby carrots

Directions:
1. Preheat the oven to 375 degrees F.
2. Place diced celery root in a medium bowl and add 1 teaspoon of olive oil, black pepper, and rosemary. Toss until celery root is fully coated before placing into baking dish.
3. Bake in the oven for 45 minutes, until golden brown.
4. Place the carrots in a medium bowl and add 1 teaspoon of olive oil. Toss until carrots are fully coated. Put the mixture in a baking dish and bake in the oven for 30 minutes. (This can be started 15 minutes after celery root had been put into oven in order to ensure equal cooking time.)
5. Once both dishes have been baked, combine in a large serving bowl and serve while hot.

Nutritional Information (Per Serving)
Calories: 88

Fat: 2.8 g
Sat Fat: 0.4 g
Carbohydrates: 15.2 g
Fiber: 3.7 g
Sugar: 4.5 g
Protein: 2.1 g
Sodium: 158 mg

Green Olive and Pork Quesadillas

Yield: 6 servings
Ingredients:
1 large onion, chopped
3 cloves garlic, minced garlic
2 teaspoons chili powder
½ teaspoon ground cumin
¼ teaspoon ground cinnamon
¼ teaspoon dried oregano, crushed
2 tablespoons sugar-free chocolate pieces
1 medium red onion, thinly sliced
3 tablespoons pimiento-stuffed green olives, sliced
2 teaspoons flour
⅓ cup water
1½ pounds ground pork, cooked
6 flour tortillas
Olive oil spray
¾ cup shredded Parmesan cheese

Directions:
1. Spray olive oil on an unheated, large skillet. Cook the onion and garlic over medium heat for about 4 minutes or until translucent.
2. Stir in chili powder, cumin, cinnamon, and oregano. Cook for 1 minute more.
3. Stir in flour. Stir in water. Cook until thick and bubbly, mixing continuously.
4. Add chocolate, stir until melted. Add ground pork and simmer lightly.
5. Spray oil on one side of each tortilla. Layout the tortillas, sprayed sides down on waxed paper. Sprinkle cheese on half of each tortilla. Spread pork on tortillas evenly. Add red onion and green olives. Fold in the tortillas to make half-moons. Press lightly.

6. Preheat oven to 300 degrees F.

7. Cook quesadillas two at a time in a skillet over medium heat for 4–6 minutes or until lightly brown. Remove quesadillas from skillet. Place on baking sheet in heated oven to keep warm.

8. Cut each quesadilla into wedges and serve.

Nutritional Information (Per Serving)
Calories: 294
Fat: 9.2 g
Sat Fat: 4.3 g
Carbohydrates: 17.4 g
Fiber: 2.8 g
Sugar: 1.4 g
Protein: 36.3 g
Sodium: 220 mg

ıch Salad with Shrimp

ıld: 3 servings

Ingredients:
4 tablespoons olive oil
3 tablespoons red wine vinegar
1 tablespoon spicy mustard
1 garlic clove, minced
Salt and pepper to taste
1 cup small salad shrimp, cooked and chilled
12 ounces fresh baby spinach
½ cup grape tomatoes, halved
¼ cup sliced red onion
½ cup sliced mushrooms
¼ cup chopped walnuts

Directions:
1. In a bowl, whisk together the oil, vinegar, mustard, garlic, salt, and pepper. Add the shrimp and toss until it's all coated.
2. In a large bowl, toss together the spinach, tomatoes, onion, and mushrooms.
3. Add the shrimp to the bowl and toss everything together.
4. Top with the walnuts.

Nutritional Information (Per Serving)
Calories: 400
Fat: 27.2 g
Sat Fat: 3.7 g
Carbohydrates: 10.7 g
Fiber: 3.9 g
Sugar: 3.1 g
Protein: 31.1 g

Turkey and Spinach Salad

Yield: 1 serving

Ingredients:

2 cups baby spinach, fresh
½ cup whole baby beets, thinly sliced
1½ ounces low-sodium smoked turkey breast, sliced in strips
¼ cup blueberries
2 tablespoons red onion, thinly sliced
2 tablespoons grated Parmesan cheese
1 tablespoon fresh orange juice
1 tablespoons apple cider vinegar
2 teaspoons olive oil

Directions:

1. Lay the spinach out on a plate. Top with the sliced beets, turkey strips, blueberries, red onion, and Parmesan cheese.

2. For the dressing, combine orange juice, vinegar, and oil in a small container. Cover tightly and shake.

3. Sprinkle dressing generously over salad mix.

Nutritional Information (Per Serving)
Calories: 293
Fat: 16.7 g
Sat Fat: 4.1 g
Carbohydrates: 20.1 g
Fiber: 3.7 g
Sugar: 9.1 g
Protein: 17.8 g
Sodium: 851 mg

Green Bean and Anchovy Salad

Yield: 3 servings
Ingredients:
1 pound fresh green beans
1 can anchovies, rinsed
2 cloves garlic, minced
¼ cup olive oil

Directions:
1. Rinse and trim the green beans.
2. Heat a pot of water until it's boiling. Add the green beans and cook for 5 minutes, then rinse.
3. In another pot, heat the olive oil and add the anchovies and the garlic. Use a wooden spoon to break down the anchovies until they dissolve into the oil.
4. Toss the anchovies and oil with the green beans.

Nutritional Information (Per Serving)
Calories: 225
Fat: 18.5 g
Sat Fat: 2.8 g
Carbohydrates: 11.4 g
Fiber: 5.2 g
Sugar: 2.1 g
Protein: 7.2 g
Sodium: 560 mg

Spicy Tomato Couscous

Yield: 8 servings
Ingredients:
8 large beefsteak tomatoes
1 tablespoon olive oil
½ cup couscous
1 cup low-salt vegetable broth
½ cup almonds, chopped
1 small eggplant, cut into ½-inch squares
1 teaspoon ground coriander
½ teaspoon ground cumin
Pinch of ground cinnamon
2 tablespoons fresh mint, chopped
½ cup dried apricots, chopped
1 teaspoon harissa paste***
Salt and pepper to taste

*** Harissa is a fiery hot condiment made from a combination of chili peppers, garlic, coriander, cumin, caraway, and olive oil. Just a dash gives the couscous the perfect kick.

Directions:
1. Slice tops off the tomatoes and remove the insides using a teaspoon. Set hollow tomatoes aside.
2. Using a sieve, extract juices from scooped-out tomato meat until you have 4 tablespoons of juice. Set aside.
3. Sprinkle a small amount of salt on insides of the tomatoes. Turn upside down on a plate covered with paper towel. Allow to drain while making couscous.
4. Spray or drizzle a small amount of olive oil in a non-stick pan and heat. Place the almonds and cook until golden brown, about 2 minutes. Remove from pan and set aside.
5. Sprinkle the pan with olive oil once more. Put the eggplant in pan and cook until brown and tender, about 5

minutes. Turn frequently to prevent burning. Add cumin, coriander, and cinnamon and cook for a few seconds, stirring constantly.

6. Pour in the broth and increase heat. When boiling, add couscous in increments, stirring continuously. Remove broth from heat, cover, and let stand for 5 minutes.

7. Uncover the pan. Cook on low heat for 2 minutes. Stir continuously with fork to separate couscous grains and make them fluffy. Add almonds, mint, and dried apricots.

8. Lastly, mix harissa paste with the tomato juice set aside from earlier. Pour the spicy juice over couscous. Season as desired.

9. Put couscous mixture inside the hollow tomatoes. Return tops and serve.

Nutritional Information (Per Serving)
Calories: 144
Fat: 5.4 g
Sat Fat: 0.5 g
Carbohydrates: 21.6 g
Fiber: 5.8 g
Sugar: 7.9 g
Protein: 5 g
Sodium: 29 mg

Easy Chicken Taco Pizzas

Yield: 4 servings
Ingredients:
2 whole wheat pita breads
1 teaspoon olive oil
2 cups cooked chicken breast, cut into squares
¼ cup bottled salsa
1 cup shredded Parmesan cheese
1½ cups lettuce, shredded
2/3 cup chopped tomatoes
Light sour cream

Directions:
For the topping:
1. Preheat oven to 425 degrees F.
2. Place pita bread cut side up on ungreased baking sheet. Brush tops of each piece with oil. Bake for 4 minutes or until pita is lightly browned and crisp.
3. Mix the chicken and salsa. Spoon chicken mixture over pita bread pieces. Sprinkle lightly with cheese.
4. Bake again for about 5 minutes or until chicken is warm and cheese has melted.
5. Top with lettuce and sprinkle with tomatoes. Drizzle with light sour cream.

Nutritional Information (Per Serving)
Calories: 343
Fat: 13.7 g
Sat Fat: 5.8 g
Carbohydrates: 23.1 g
Fiber: 3.5 g
Sugar: 2.3 g
Protein: 33.9 g
Sodium: 583 mg

Rosemary Chicken Wrap

Yield: 2 servings
Ingredients:
10 ounces cooked chicken breast
2 whole-grain tortillas
2 cups kale
2 tablespoons plain Greek yogurt
¼ cup roasted red peppers, chopped
¼ cup cucumbers, chopped
2 tablespoons olive oil
2 tablespoons balsamic vinegar
2 tablespoons slivered almonds
2 sprigs of fresh rosemary
Salt and pepper to taste

Directions:
1. Chop up the chicken breast, and toss with oil, vinegar, fresh rosemary, and almonds.
2. Spread out each tortilla. Spread one tablespoon of yogurt onto each wrap, and then cover with kale.
3. Add the chicken mixture on top of the kale, and then add the cucumbers and red peppers.
4. Sprinkle with salt and pepper, and roll the wraps so that they can be held by hand.

Nutritional Information (Per Serving)
Calories: 574
Fat: 27.7 g
Sat Fat: 4.7 g
Carbohydrates: 38.5 g
Fiber: 9.8 g
Sugar: 5.0 g
Protein: 44.9 g

Breadless Bruschetta

Yield: 1 serving

Ingredients:
2 tomatoes, seeded and chopped
¼ cup fresh basil, chopped
1 clove garlic, minced
¼ cup red onion, chopped
1 tablespoon olive oil
1 tablespoon balsamic vinegar
1 cucumber, sliced into thick pieces
Salt and pepper to taste

Directions:
1. Mix everything together except for cucumber.
2. Once bruschetta mixture has been combined, spoon mixture on top of cucumber slices.

Nutritional Information (Per Serving)
Calories: 230
Fat: 14.9 g
Sat Fat: 2.2 g
Carbohydrates: 24.5 g
Fiber: 5.2 g
Sugar: 12.8 g
Protein: 4.8 g

Quinoa and Black Beans

Yield: 6 servings

Ingredients:
1 teaspoon vegetable oil
1 chopped onion
3 cloves garlic, chopped
¾ cup quinoa
1½ cups vegetable broth
1 teaspoon ground cumin
¼ teaspoon cayenne pepper
3 cups canned black beans, drained
½ cup cilantro

Directions:
1. In a sauce pan, warm vegetable oil over medium heat. Add the onion and garlic and cook until slightly brown, approximately 5 minutes.
2. Mix the quinoa into onion mixture and cover with vegetable broth. Season the mixture with cayenne pepper, cumin, and pepper.
3. Bring the mixture to a boil then cover, reduce heat, and simmer until quinoa is tender and has absorbed the broth, approximately 20 minutes.
4. Mix in black beans and cilantro.

Nutritional Information (Per Serving)
Calories: 187
Fat: 3.9 g
Sat Fat: 0.7 g
Carbohydrates: 26.4 g
Fiber: 5.5 g
Sugar: 2 g
Protein: 11.3 g
Sodium: 708 mg

Fish and Squash Meal

Yield: 4 servings

Ingredients:
1 teaspoon grated lemon peel
1 red onion, chopped
1 cup zucchini, cut into squares
1 cup squash, cut into squares
1 teaspoon minced garlic
4 fish fillets, sliced 1 inch thick
2 tablespoons fresh mint leaves, finely chopped
1 tablespoon red wine vinegar
2 tablespoons extra virgin olive oil
1 tablespoon water

Directions:
1. Preheat oven to 400 degrees F.
2. In a baking dish, combine grated lemon, 1 tablespoon of oil, and onions. Spread on dish evenly. Bake in oven until onion is translucent for about 15 minutes, stirring occasionally.
3. Remove from oven. Add the zucchini, squash, and garlic and mix. Make sure it's spread evenly before returning to oven to bake for another 10 minutes.
4. Remove from oven once cooked.
5. Increase oven temperature to 450 degrees F. Move vegetables to one side and add fish fillets. Spoon vegetables over fish.
6. Return the dish to the oven and bake until fish is flaky, 10 minutes for thin fillets and 15 minutes for thicker fillets.
7. In a small bowl, combine remaining oil with vinegar, water, mint leaves, and onion.
5. Spoon the spice mixture over fillets and serve.

Nutritional Information (Per Serving)

Calories: 295
Fat: 18.3 g
Sat Fat: 3.6 g
Carbohydrates: 20.7 g
Fiber: 2 g
Sugar: 2.3 g
Protein: 14.5 g
Sodium: 493 mg

Grilled Vegetables

Yield: 4 servings

Ingredients:
¼ cup olive oil
4 teaspoons balsamic vinegar
2 tablespoons honey
1 teaspoon dried oregano
1 teaspoon ground cumin
½ teaspoon garlic powder
Salt and pepper to taste
4 small carrots, peeled and halved lengthwise
1 medium zucchini, cut into ½" slices
1 large red bell pepper, seeded and cut into 1" strips
1 pound fresh asparagus, trimmed
1 medium red onion, cut into wedges

Directions:

1. In a small bowl, mix together all ingredients except vegetables.

2. In a large bowl, add 3 tablespoons of the marinade mixture, reserving the remaining.

3. Add vegetables to the bowl, and toss to coat well. Set aside, covered for about 1½ hours.

4. Preheat the grill to medium heat. Grease the grill grate.

5. Arrange the vegetables over grill grate in a single layer. Grill, covered for 8–12 minutes, flipping occasionally.

Nutritional Information (Per Serving)
Calories: 218
Fat: 13.1 g
Sat Fat: 1.9 g
Carbohydrates: 25 g
Fiber: 5.7 g
Sugar: 16.9 g

Protein: 4.3 g

These diabetic lunch recipes will help you keep your blood sugar under control and provide you with the vitamins and nutrients you need to stay healthy. When you make healthy choices, managing your diabetes will be a lot easier.

Chapter 4: Diabetic Friendly Snacks

Snacks are an important part of any diet, even if it's a diabetic one. They serve a physical purpose, which is to prevent you from getting too hungry and to keep your blood sugar regulated. They also serve a mental purpose—snacking is something that nearly everyone enjoys doing.

Snacks don't mean sweets. The ideal snack contains only 15 to 30 grams of carbs and between 100 to 200 calories. The snacks in this chapter are delicious and will give you an energy boost at the same time.

Snacks with less than 5 grams of Carbohydrates:
5 baby carrots
2 saltine crackers
¼ of an avocado (You can turn this into a smoothie snack)
1 hard boiled egg
1 sugar free popsicle
15 almonds

Snacks with 10 to 20 grams of carbohydrates:
Hummus with veggies
1 cup of fresh or canned fruit (without syrup)
1 small apple
1 cup soup (chicken noodle, tomato or vegetable soup)
½ cup nuts or dried fruit mix.

Snacks with 30 grams of carbohydrates:
1 English muffin
¾ cup whole grain cereal with ½ cup non-fat milk
1 banana coated with 1 tablespoon peanut butter
6 ounces non-fat yogurt with ¾ cup of any berry

Tuna on Cukes

Yield: 2 servings
Ingredients:
1 can tuna packed in water
1 cucumber
1 tablespoon mayonnaise
½ stalk celery, chopped
2 tablespoons red onion, minced
1 teaspoon dried basil
1 teaspoon dried oregano
¼ cup fresh sprouts
Salt and pepper to taste

Directions:
1. Slice the cucumber into thick rounds and sprinkle with salt and pepper.
2. Combine the tuna, mayonnaise, celery, onion, and herbs. Mix together. Spoon by the tablespoon onto the cucumber pieces and top with fresh sprouts.
3. Add additional salt and pepper if desired.

Nutritional Information (Per Serving)
Calories: 224
Fat: 9.9 g
Sat Fat: 1.9 g
Carbohydrates: 8.8 g
Fiber: 1.4 g
Sugar: 3.5 g
Protein: 24.9 g

Roasted Seeds and Nuts

Yield: 15 servings
Ingredients:
1 cup almonds
1 cup walnuts
1 cup hazelnuts
1 cup peanuts
½ cup pumpkin seeds
¼ cup sunflower seeds
¼ cup pine nuts
2 sprigs of fresh rosemary
6 leaves of fresh sage
1 teaspoon cayenne pepper
1 tablespoon olive oil
Salt and pepper to taste

Directions:
1. Preheat the oven to 400 degrees F.
2. Spread the nuts and seeds evenly on baking sheet. Sprinkle with cayenne pepper, olive oil, salt, and pepper. Add rosemary and sage.
3. Roast in the oven for about 20 minutes. Remove and allow to cool.

Nutritional Information (Per Serving)
Calories: 228
Fat: 20.9 g
Sat Fat: 2.1 g
Carbohydrates: 6 g
Fiber: 3.1 g
Sugar: 1.1 g
Protein: 8.2 g

Stuffed Mushrooms

Yield: 4 servings
Ingredients:
1 pound mushrooms
½ cup chicken broth
8 ounces Boursin cheese
Paprika to garnish

Directions:
1. Preheat the oven to 350 degrees F.
2. Remove the stems from the mushrooms, and reserve them for another use.
3. Fill all the mushrooms with Boursin cheese, and place them in a baking pan.
4. Pour some chicken broth around the mushrooms to fill the bottom of the pan. Sprinkle with paprika.
5. Bake for 30–40 minutes and serve hot.

Nutritional Information (Per Serving)
Calories: 256
Fat: 25 g
Sat Fat: 17.1 g
Carbohydrates: 5.7 g
Fiber: 1.1 g
Sugar: 3.9 g
Protein: 8 g
Sodium: 442 mg

Celery Zucchini Smoothie

Smoothies are great snacks. They are delicious, nutritious, and low in calories. Use non-fat milk and avoid fruits like mango.

Yield: 2 servings

Ingredients:
1 celery stalk, chopped
1 tablespoon lime juice
1 banana, sliced
¼ cup zucchini
½ bunch of parsley
2 cups of water
½ cup ice

Directions:
Blend all ingredients until the mixture is smooth.

Nutritional Information (Per Serving)
Calories: 66
Fat: 0.4 g
Sat Fat: 0.1 g
Carbohydrates: 16.4 g
Fiber: 2.6 g
Sugar: 8.1 g
Protein: 1.4 g
Sodium: 27 mg

Bitter Berry Smoothie

Yield: 1 serving
Ingredients:
1 cup strawberries
1 small size bitter melon, seeded and chopped
½ cup soy milk
½ cup ice
Honey to taste

Directions:
Reap the benefits of bitter melon to keep your blood sugar stable with this awesome smoothie. Put all ingredients in a blender and blend until smooth.

Nutritional Information (Per Serving)
Calories: 125
Fat: 2.6 g
Sat Fat: 0.3 g
Carbohydrates: 21.3 g
Fiber: 4.1 g
Sugar: 12 g
Protein: 5.5 g
Sodium: 69 mg

Apple Pie Smoothie

Yield: 2 servings
Ingredients:
1 cup coconut milk
1 apple, peeled, cored, and sliced
1 tablespoon almond butter
½ tablespoon ground chia seeds
1 teaspoon ground cinnamon
1 cup ice

Directions:
Use any kind of apple that's local, seasonal, and flavorful. Combine all ingredients in a blender and whip it all together.

Nutritional Information (Per Serving)
Calories: 405
Fat: 35.4 g
Sat Fat: 26 g
Carbohydrates: 23.3 g
Fiber: 9.3 g
Sugar: 12.4 g
Protein: 6.3 g
Sodium: 20 mg

t Potato Fries

ield: 2 servings

ingredients:

1 large sweet potato, peeled and cut into wedges
1 teaspoon ground turmeric
1 teaspoon ground cinnamon
2 tablespoons extra virgin olive oil
Salt and pepper to taste

Directions:

1. Preheat the oven to 425 degrees F.
2. In a large bowl, add all ingredients, and toss to coat well.
3. Line a baking sheet with foil. Transfer the sweet potato mixture onto the baking sheet.
4. Bake for about 25 minutes, flipping once after 15 minutes.
5. Serve immediately.

Nutritional Information (Per Serving)
Calories: 208
Fat: 14.3 g
Sat Fat: 2 g
Carbohydrates: 20.3 g
Fiber: 3.8 g
Sugar: 5.9 g
Protein: 2 g

Carrot Cake Cookies

Yield: 18 servings

Ingredients:

½ cup honey

¼ cup brown sugar or equivalent brown sugar substitute of choice

1 tablespoon butter, softened

¼ cup canola oil

1 egg

1 egg white

3 cups carrots, grated

2 cups all-purpose white flour

½ cup whole wheat flour

1 teaspoon pumpkin pie spice blend

½ teaspoon baking powder

½ teaspoon baking soda

¼ teaspoon salt

¾ cup chopped walnuts

2 ounces reduced-fat cream or Neufchatel cheese, softened

½ cup confectioner's sugar

3 tablespoons milk

Directions:

1. Preheat oven to 350 degrees F.
2. Grease 2 cookie sheets or line with parchment paper.
3. In a large bowl, combine honey, brown sugar, and butter. Beat well with an electric mixer. Beat in oil, egg, and egg white. Stir in carrots.
4. In a separate bowl, mix flours, baking powder, baking soda, and salt. Gradually add to carrot mixture, stirring well. Stir in walnuts.

5. Using a tablespoon, place mounds on cookie sheets, 2 inches apart. Bake for 10–12 minutes or until lightly browned.

6. Transfer to wire racks to cool.

7. Once cool, make a drizzle to go on top. Combine cream cheese, confectioner's sugar, and milk and beat well. Drizzle over top of cookies before serving. Cookies may be sprinkled with additional chopped walnuts if desired.

Nutritional Information (Per Serving)
Calories: 199
Fat: 7.9 g
Sat Fat: 1.4 g
Carbohydrates: 28.9 g
Fiber: 1.3 g
Sugar: 14.2 g
Protein: 4.1 g
Sodium: 104 mg

Oven Baked Grapefruit

Yield: 2 servings
Ingredients:
1 grapefruit, medium-sized
½ teaspoon ground cinnamon
1 Splenda packet (or comparable sugar substitute)

Directions:
1. Preheat oven to 400 degrees F.
2. Cut grapefruit in half horizontally, using a sharp knife. Using a serrated knife or a grapefruit spoon, loosen segments of fruit, but do not remove from skin.
3. Place halves cut side up on a baking sheet. Sprinkle evenly with cinnamon and sugar substitute. Place in oven and bake for about 20 minutes, or until warmed.
4. Let cool for about 5 minutes before serving. Eat with a grapefruit spoon or serrated spoon or cut up before serving.

Nutritional Information (Per Serving)
Calories: 22
Fat: 0.1 g
Sat Fat: 0 g
Carbohydrates: 5.6 g
Fiber: 1 g
Sugar: 4.5 g
Protein: 0.4 g
Sodium: 0 mg

Edamame and Guacamole

Yield: 6 servings
Ingredients:
2 avocados
1 cup tomatoes, diced
1 clove garlic, minced
¼ cup red onion, diced
8 ounces edamame, steamed
½ lime, juiced
½ teaspoon cayenne pepper
Salt and pepper to taste

Directions:
1. Peel the avocados and remove the pit. Smash it with a fork and stir in the tomatoes, garlic, and red onion.
2. Add the lime juice and cayenne pepper. Sprinkle with salt and pepper.
3. Use the edamame to scoop up the guacamole. Other veggies will work well as dippers too.

Nutritional Information (Per Serving)
Calories: 202
Fat: 15.7 g
Sat Fat: 3.1 g
Carbohydrates: 12.4 g
Fiber: 6.8 g
Sugar: 1.5 g
Protein: 6.6 g

Spicy Popcorn

Yield: 2 servings

Ingredients:
2 tablespoons coconut oil
½ cup popping corn
1 tablespoon olive oil
1 teaspoon ground turmeric
⅛ teaspoon ground cinnamon
Salt to taste

Directions:
1. In a pan, melt coconut oil over medium-high heat.
2. Add popping corn, and cover the pan tightly.
3. Cook, shaking the pan every 10 seconds until popping slows down.
4. Remove from heat, and transfer into a large heatproof bowl. Add olive oil and spices, and mix well.
5. Serve immediately

Nutritional Information (Per Serving)
Calories: 212
Fat: 21 g
Sat Fat: 12.8 g
Carbohydrates: 8.3 g
Fiber: 1.2 g
Sugar: 1.2 g
Protein: 1.1 g

Pumpkin Bars

Yield: 25 servings

Ingredients:

½ cup softened butter

½ cup brown sugar (sugar substitutes are not recommended with this recipe)

½ teaspoon baking soda

½ teaspoon pumpkin pie spice

⅓ cup canned pumpkin

1 egg

1½ cups all-purpose flour

4 ounces cream cheese, softened

1 cup whipped cream

Nutmeg

Directions:

1. Preheat oven to 350 degrees F.
2. Lightly grease and flour a 9x9x2-inch baking dish and set aside.
3. Mix together baking soda, brown sugar, butter, and pumpkin pie spice in a big bowl. Beat the mixture with an electric mixer on medium speed until well-mixed. Add pumpkin and egg. Beat in as much flour as possible. Not all flour will be added in this fashion; the rest must be stirred in using wooden spoon.
4. Spread this dough into the prepared baking dish. Bake for 12 to 15 minutes (until a wooden toothpick can be inserted into the center and come out clean).
5. Let cool for 10 minutes before removing dessert from the dish. Allow to cool.
6. In a medium bowl, use a mixer on medium speed to beat the cream cheese until smooth. Beat in the whipped cream.

7. Spread the mixture over top of the dessert. Sprinkle with nutmeg before cutting into bars.

Nutritional Information (Per Bar)
Calories: 177
Fat: 7.2 g
Sat Fat: 4.4 g
Carbohydrates: 24.4 g
Fiber: 0.8 g
Sugar: 3 g
Protein: 3.6 g
Sodium: 44 mg

When you're making diabetic-friendly snacks, the key is to use healthy and fresh ingredients whenever possible and to limit serving size. The purpose of a snack isn't to fill you up, but to curb cravings and keep your blood sugar balanced. Make sure your snack portions don't get out of control and grow to the size of a meal.

Chapter 5: Diabetic Dinner Recipes

Dinner is a meal best served hot. At the end of the day, you want to have a delicious but light meal. In diabetics, blood sugars usually rise when they wake up while the body processes their evening meals. Keeping it light will help keep your sugar levels low.

Rosemary Chicken and Rice

Yield: 4 servings
Ingredients:
1 pound chicken tenders
2 sprigs fresh rosemary
1 lemon, juiced
2 tablespoons olive oil
2 stalks celery
Salt and pepper to taste
2 cups cooked brown rice

Directions:
1. Preheat the oven to 350 degrees F.
2. Toss the chicken tenders with olive oil, salt, and pepper. Layer into a baking dish and top with celery and rosemary sprigs.
3. Squeeze the juice of a lemon over the dish.
4. Bake in the oven for 20 minutes, while your brown rice cooks.
5. Remove chicken from the oven and chop it into pieces. Chop the celery as well.
6. Remove rosemary from the stems and toss everything into the pot with the rice to combine.

Nutritional Information (Per Serving)

Calories: 356
Fat: 16 g
Sat Fat: 3.3 g
Carbohydrates: 17.4 g
Fiber: 0.7 g
Sugar: 1.5 g
Protein: 34.4 g

Spicy Chicken Stew

Yield: 6 servings

Ingredients:
2 tablespoons olive oil
1 onion, chopped
½ tablespoon fresh ginger, grated finely
1 tablespoon fresh garlic, minced
1 teaspoon ground coriander
1 teaspoon paprika
1 teaspoon cayenne pepper
6 skinless, boneless chicken thighs, trimmed and cut into 1" pieces
3 Roma tomatoes, chopped
1 cup coconut milk
1 cup chicken broth
⅓ cup fresh cilantro, chopped
Salt and pepper to taste

Directions:
1. In a large pan, heat oil over medium heat. Add onion and sauté for 3 minutes.
2. Add ginger, garlic, and spices, and sauté for 1 minute.
3. Add chicken and cook for 4–5 minutes.
4. Add tomatoes, coconut milk, broth, salt, and pepper, and bring to a gentle simmer.
5. Reduce the heat to low and simmer, covered for about 10–15 minutes or until desired doneness.
6. Stir in cilantro, and remove from heat.

Nutritional Information (Per Serving)
Calories: 167
Fat: 8.8 g
Sat Fat: 2.3 g
Carbohydrates: 7.4 g

Fiber: 1.1 g
Sugar: 4.3 g
Protein: 14.8 g

Chicken with Parmesan Crust

Yield: 2 servings

Ingredients:
3 tablespoons dried bread crumbs
2 tablespoons Parmesan cheese, grated
1 tablespoon fresh parsley, minced
1 teaspoon dried oregano
¼ teaspoon salt
¼ teaspoon paprika
¼ teaspoon pepper
1 tablespoon butter, melted
2 skinless chicken breasts (8 ounces each)

Directions:
1. Preheat oven to 350 degrees F.
2. In a shallow plate, combine the first seven ingredients. Mix well.
3. Brush the chicken with the melted butter and coat with the crumb mixture. Place in an 11x7 inch baking dish coated with cooking spray.
4. Bake without cover in the oven for 45–50 minutes, or until a meat thermometer reads 170.

Nutritional Information (Per Serving)
Calories: 518
Fat: 16 g
Sat Fat: 8.8 g
Carbohydrates: 16.5 g
Fiber: 1 g
Sugar: 0.7 g
Protein: 75.9 g
Sodium: 472 mg

Ginger Steak

Yield: 4 servings

Ingredients:
8 garlic cloves, crushed
2 teaspoons fresh ginger, sliced thinly
1 tablespoon honey
¼ cup olive oil
Salt and freshly ground black pepper to taste
1½ pounds flank steak, trimmed

Directions:
1. In a large sealable bag, mix together all ingredients except steak.
2. Add steak and coat generously with marinade.
3. Seal the bag, and refrigerate to marinate for about 24 hours.
4. Remove the steak from refrigerator, and keep at room temperature for about 15 minutes.
5. Heat a lightly greased grill pan over medium-high heat. Discard the excess marinade from steak, and place the steak in the grill pan.
7. Cook for 6–8 minutes on each side or until desired doneness.
8. Remove from grill pan, and cool for 10 minutes before slicing.
9. With a sharp knife, cut into desired slices and serve.

Nutritional Information (Per Serving)
Calories: 407
Fat: 26.2 g
Sat Fat: 7.3 g
Carbohydrates: 6.5 g
Fiber: 0.2 g
Sugar: 4.4 g
Protein: 35 g

Sautéed Spicy Shrimp

Yield: 6 servings

Ingredients:
1 pound shrimp, shell and veins removed
½ cup low-salt chicken broth
1 tablespoon soy sauce, light
¼ teaspoon red pepper flakes, finely crushed
3 cups frozen mixed vegetables
3 cups brown rice, cooked
2 tablespoons corn starch
Olive oil spray

Directions:

1. Mix chicken broth and corn starch in a small bowl until dissolved. Add soy sauce and red pepper flakes.

2. Spray a large, nonstick skillet with oil and increase to medium heat. Add the frozen vegetables and cook until vegetables are thawed.

3. Add the chicken broth and bring to a simmer. Add the shrimp and cook until shrimp is pinkish-red.

4. Serve over brown rice.

Nutritional Information (Per Serving)
Calories: 238
Fat: 1.9 g
Sat Fat: 0.4 g
Carbohydrates: 32.3 g
Fiber: 4.5 g
Sugar: 2.9 g
Protein: 21.7 g
Sodium: 418 mg

Bitter Melon Curry

Yield: 2 servings
Ingredients:
3 small bitter melons
½ cup grated coconut
¼ teaspoon cumin
1 cup yogurt
½ teaspoon turmeric powder
½ teaspoon mustard
A few curry leaves
6 teaspoons coconut oil
¼ teaspoon sugar
Salt to taste

Directions:

1. Wash the bitter melons, remove seeds, and slice into thin slices.

2. Heat 4 teaspoons of coconut oil in frying pan. Fry the bitter melons until crisp and brown. Salt to taste and set aside.

3. Combine the coconut, cumin, and turmeric powders before adding to the yogurt. In the frying pan, heat the mixture until it begins to boil.

4. In another pan, heat 2 teaspoons coconut oil with mustard until it starts to crackle, then add curry leaves to fry. Pour the curry leaves into the yogurt mixture to make a curry.

5. Allow the bitter melon and curry to cool slightly before mixing them together, adding the sugar before serving. This curry can be served with rice.

Nutritional Information (Per Serving)
Calories: 296
Fat: 22.2 g
Sat Fat: 18.9 g

Carbohydrates: 15.9 g
Fiber: 2.1 g
Sugar: 10.5 g
Protein: 8.5 g
Sodium: 92 mg

Meatballs Curry

Yield: 6 servings
Ingredients:
For Meatballs:
1 pound lean ground turkey
2 eggs, beaten
3 tablespoons red onion, minced
¼ cup fresh basil leaves, chopped
¼ teaspoon fresh ginger, chopped finely
4 garlic cloves, chopped finely
1 jalapeño pepper, seeded and minced
1 tablespoon red curry paste
1 tablespoon fish sauce
2 tablespoons coconut oil
Salt to taste

For Curry:
1 red onion, chopped
4 garlic cloves, minced
½ teaspoon fresh ginger, minced
1 jalapeño pepper, seeded and minced
2 tablespoons red curry paste
1 (14 ounces) can coconut milk
2 tablespoons fresh lime juice
Salt and pepper to taste

Directions:
1. For meatballs, in a large bowl, add all ingredients except oil, and mix until well combined. Make small balls from the mixture.
2. In a large skillet, melt coconut oil over medium heat. Add meatballs and cook for 3–5 minutes or until golden brown on all sides. Transfer the meatballs into a bowl.

3. In the same skillet, add onion and a pinch of salt, and sauté for 3 minutes.

4. Add garlic, ginger, and jalapeño, and sauté for 1 minute.

5. Add curry paste, and sauté for 1 minute.

6. Add coconut milk and meatballs, and bring to a gentle simmer. Reduce heat to low and simmer, covered for about 10 minutes.

7. Serve with a drizzling of lime juice.

Nutritional Information (Per Serving)
Calories: 370
Fat: 29.5 g
Sat Fat: 20.8 g
Carbohydrates: 9.8 g
Fiber: 2.2 g
Sugar: 3.7 g
Protein: 19 g

Chili Beef Pasta

Yield: 6 servings

Ingredients:
8 ounces whole wheat spiral pasta
1 pound lean ground beef
1 can (6 ounces) tomato paste
2 tablespoons minced onion, dried
2 teaspoons dried oregano
2 teaspoons chili powder
½ teaspoon garlic powder
⅛ teaspoon salt
3 cups tomato juice
2 cups water

Directions:

1. In a large skillet, cook the ground beef over medium heat for 6 to 8 minutes or until slightly brown. Separate beef with a fork. Drain. Add the seasonings.

2. Mix the tomato juice, water, and tomato paste in a pan. Bring to a boil.

3. Stir in the pasta. Lower heat, cover, and let simmer for 20 minutes or until pasta is tender. Stir occasionally to keep pasta from overcooking.

4. Serve hot.

Nutritional Information (Per Serving)
Calories: 330
Fat: 5.8 g
Sat Fat: 2 g
Carbohydrates: 39.7 g
Fiber: 5.9 g
Sugar: 14.0 g
Protein: 9.9 g
Sodium: 464 mg

Spicy Lamb with Peas

Yield: 4 servings
Ingredients:
1 tablespoon coconut oil
3 dried red chilies
1 (2") cinnamon stick
3 green cardamom pods
1 medium red onion, chopped
½ teaspoon fresh ginger, minced
4 garlic cloves, minced
1½ teaspoons ground coriander
½ teaspoon garam masala
½ teaspoon ground cumin
½ teaspoon ground turmeric
2 bay leaves
1 pound lean ground lamb
½ cup Roma tomatoes, chopped
1½ cups water
1 cup fresh green peas, shelled
¼ cup fresh cilantro, chopped
Salt and pepper to taste

Directions:
1. In a Dutch oven, melt coconut oil over medium-high heat. Add red chilies, cinnamon stick, and cardamom pods, and sauté for about 30 seconds.
2. Add onion and sauté for about 3–4 minutes. Add ginger, garlic cloves, and spices, and sauté for 30 seconds.
3. Add lamb and cook for 5 minutes.
4. Add tomatoes and cook for about 10 minutes.
5. Stir in water and green peas, and cook, covered for about 20 minutes.
6. Stir in cilantro, salt, and pepper, and remove from heat.

7. Serve hot.

Nutritional Information (Per Serving)
Calories: 298
Fat: 12.2 g
Sat Fat: 6 g
Carbohydrates: 11.3 g
Fiber: 3.4 g
Sugar: 4.1 g
Protein: 34.8 g

Spicy Turkey and Beans

Yield: 4 servings
Ingredients:
4 turkey breast cutlets
2 teaspoons paprika
1 teaspoon cumin
1 teaspoon dried oregano
2 tablespoons olive oil
1 cup red onion, chopped
1 cup red bell pepper, chopped
½ cup frozen peas
½ cup black beans, drained and rinsed
Salt and pepper to taste

Directions:
1. In a small bowl, mix the paprika, cumin, and oregano.
2. Season the turkey cutlets with salt and pepper, then rub each side with the spice mixture.
3. In a large skillet, heat the oil. Add the onion and bell pepper. Cook for 5 minutes.
4. Add any remaining spice mixture to the vegetables. Stir in the frozen peas and the beans. Cook for 5 minutes and then set aside.
5. In the same skillet, cook the turkey for 3 minutes on each side. Serve on top of beans.

Nutritional Information (Per Serving)
Calories: 306
Fat: 8.3 g
Sat Fat: 1.1 g
Carbohydrates: 24 g
Fiber: 6.4 g
Sugar: 4.3 g
Protein: 35.2 g

Thai Turkey Paleo Mix

Yield: 2 servings
Ingredients:
½ pound ground turkey
4 tablespoons fresh lime juice
2 tablespoons tahini
1 tablespoon apple cider vinegar
1 teaspoon grated ginger
1 clove garlic, grated
6" pieces lemongrass, sliced into coins
1 tablespoon canola oil
Pinch of cayenne (optional)

For the salad:
2 cups spinach, chopped
1 red bell pepper, cut into very thin strips
¼ cup red cabbage, thinly sliced
¾ cup snow peas
5 basil leaves, thinly sliced, and sprigs for garnish
¼ cup roasted peanuts, chopped

Directions:
1. Heat the oil in a skillet over medium-high heat. Add the turkey, breaking it up with a wooden spatula.
2. Add lime juice, vinegar, lemongrass, ginger, garlic, tahini, and cayenne pepper. Cook until the turkey meat is white. Remove from heat and cover.
3. Arrange the spinach, bell pepper, cabbage, and snow peas in a layer on two plates.
4. Mix the basil into the turkey mixture. Divide the turkey mix and portion onto 2 plates. Top with the salad.
5. Garnish with peanuts and basil and season with vinaigrette.

Nutritional Information (Per Serving)
Calories: 543
Fat: 37 g
Sat Fat: 5 g
Carbohydrates: 19.9 g
Fiber: 6.6 g
Sugar: 7 g
Protein: 42.2 g
Sodium: 173 mg

Turkey with Lentils and Veggies

Yield: 6 servings

Ingredients:
3 tablespoons olive oil, divided
1 onion, chopped
1 tablespoon fresh ginger, minced
4 garlic cloves, minced
3 Roma tomatoes, seeded and chopped finely
3 celery stalks, chopped
1 large carrot, peeled and chopped
1 cup dried red lentils, rinsed, soaked for 30 minutes and drained
2 cups chicken broth
1½ teaspoons cumin seeds
½ teaspoon cayenne pepper
1 pound lean ground turkey
1 jalapeño pepper, seeded and chopped
2 scallions, chopped
¼ cup fresh cilantro, chopped

Directions:
1, In a Dutch oven, heat 1 tablespoon of oil over medium heat.
2. Add onion, ginger, and garlic, and sauté for 3 minutes.
3. Stir in tomatoes, celery, carrot, lentils, and chicken broth, and bring to a boil.
4. Reduce the heat to low. Simmer, covered for about 30 minutes.
5. In a skillet, heat remaining oil over medium heat. Add cumin seeds, and sauté for 30 seconds.
6. Add paprika and sauté for 30 seconds. Transfer the mixture into a small bowl, and set aside.
7. In the same skillet, add turkey and cook for 4–5 minutes.

8. Add jalapeño and scallion, and cook for 3–4 minutes. Add spiced oil mixture, and stir to combine well.

9. Transfer the turkey mixture in simmering lentils, and simmer for 10–15 minutes or until desired doneness.

Nutritional Information (Per Serving)
Calories: 250
Fat: 13.1 g
Sat Fat: 2.9 g
Carbohydrates: 15.5 g
Fiber: 4.5 g
Sugar: 4.1 g
Protein: 19.4 g
Sodium: 407 mg

Cheesy Spinach Bake

Yield: 6 servings
Ingredients:
3 cups spinach
½ cup half & half milk
½ cup milk
3 eggs, beaten
2 egg yolks, beaten
¼ cup butter, melted
1 cup shredded cheddar cheese
2 teaspoons bread crumbs
⅛ teaspoon black pepper
Cooking spray

Directions:
1. Preheat the oven to 350 degrees F. Coat a 2-quart baking dish with cooking spray.
2. Thoroughly clean and dry the spinach before chopping it.
3. Combine cream and milk together in a medium saucepan and heat until near simmering.
4. Combine beaten eggs and yolks together in a medium bowl. Slowly add hot milk and cream, whisking continually until everything is blended together.
5. Add the melted butter slowly while constantly whisking. Add ¾ cup of shredded cheese. Fold the spinach into the dairy and cheese mixture, making sure it is well-combined.
6. Mix remaining cheese and the bread crumbs in a separate bowl. Set the mixture aside.
7. Transfer the spinach mixture into the prepared baking dish. Sprinkle the bread crumb and cheese mixture evenly over top. Bake for 30 minutes.

Nutritional Information (Per Serving)
Calories: 236
Fat: 20.4 g
Sat Fat: 11.8 g
Carbohydrates: 3.6 g
Fiber: 0.4 g
Sugar: 1.4 g
Protein: 10.2 g
Sodium: 240 mg

Twice-Baked Squash

Yield: 2 servings
Ingredients:
1 butternut squash
2 shallots, sliced
1 clove garlic, minced
¼ cup coconut milk
½ cup oats
1 tablespoon ground nutmeg
1 tablespoon olive oil
Salt and pepper to taste

Directions:
1. Preheat oven to 425 degrees F.
2. Cut the squash in half and roast for 40 minutes, until soft.
3. Heat olive oil in a skillet and cook the garlic and shallot for 5 minutes, until soft.
4. Scoop the squash out of the skin and place in a bowl. Stir in the coconut milk, shallots, and garlic. Add the oats and mix.
5. Place the mixture into the squash shells and bake for another 30 minutes.

Nutritional Information (Per Serving)
Calories: 368
Fat: 18.3 g
Sat Fat: 8.8 g
Carbohydrates: 47 g
Fiber: 8.4 g
Sugar: 5.1 g
Protein: 9.1 g

Herb Crusted Salmon with Spinach

Yield: 4 servings

Ingredients:
4 salmon fillets
2 tablespoons olive oil
1 tablespoon coriander seeds
½ teaspoon whole cloves
2 teaspoons cumin seeds
1 teaspoon fresh nutmeg, grated
Salt and pepper to taste
15 ounces fresh spinach leaves

Directions:
1. Combine the coriander, cloves, and cumin in a small bowl or a spice grinder and grind until they are in powder form.
2. Season the salmon with salt and pepper on both sides. Press the spice mixture onto the top of each piece of salmon.
3. Heat the oil in a large skillet over medium high heat. Place the salmon fillets in the pan, with the coated side on the heat.
4. Press the remaining spice mixture on top of the exposed sides of the salmon.
5. Cook on each side for about 3 minutes, until the spice coating makes a browned crust.
6. Remove the salmon and allow it to rest for a minute or two while you wilt the spinach in the same pan.

Nutritional Information (Per Serving)
Calories: 328
Fat: 18.9 g
Sat Fat: 2.8 g
Carbohydrates: 4.8 g
Fiber: 2.7 g
Sugar: 0.6 g

Protein: 37.8 g

Salmon and Asparagus

Yield: 8 servings

Ingredients:
4 skinless salmon fillets
1 cup sugar snap peas
1 tablespoon fresh chives, snipped
2 leeks, thinly sliced
8 ounces asparagus spears
4 tablespoons dry white wine
1 cup reduced-sodium vegetable broth
Salt and pepper to taste

Directions:
1. Arrange leeks in single layer in a large skillet. Coat with cooking spray. Lay the pieces of salmon on top.
2. Arrange the asparagus and peas around the fish. Sprinkle with wine and broth and season lightly with salt and pepper.
3. Heat the skillet over medium-high heat and wait for the broth to boil. Cover with tight-fitting lid and lower heat.
4. Cook until the salmon is pale pink, even on the inside, and the vegetables are tender. This will take about 12–14 minutes.
5. Once fish is ready, sprinkle with chives and serve.

Nutritional Information (Per Serving)
Calories: 244
Fat: 9.5 g
Sat Fat: 1.4 g
Carbohydrates: 5.3 g
Fiber: 1.2 g
Sugar: 1.8 g
Protein: 30.9 g

Roasted Mackerel

Yield: 4 servings
Ingredients:
8 mackerel fillets
2 garlic cloves, peeled
2 teaspoons paprika
¼ cup green onions, sliced
3 tablespoons olive oil
1 tablespoon white wine vinegar
Salt and pepper to taste

Directions:
1. Preheat oven to 400 degrees F.
2. Press the garlic and paprika together until it becomes a paste. Add some olive oil.
3. Coat the mackerel with olive oil and place on a baking sheet, skin side up. Season with salt and pepper, then cover with the garlic and paprika mixture. Sprinkle the green onions on top.
4. Bake for 10–12 minutes. Remove from the oven and drizzle with vinegar.
5. Serve with your favorite veggie.

Nutritional Information (Per Serving)
Calories: 559
Fat: 42 g
Sat Fat: 8.9 g
Carbohydrates: 1.6 g
Fiber: 0.6 g
Sugar: 0.3 g
Protein: 42.3 g

Tomato & Vegetable Quinoa Pilaf

Yield: 4 servings

Ingredients:
2 teaspoons olive oil
½ small onion, chopped
1 cup quinoa, uncooked
2 cups water
2 tablespoons chicken bouillon granules or vegetarian substitute
1 teaspoon black pepper
1 teaspoon thyme
1 carrot, chopped
1 medium tomato, chopped
1 cup baby spinach

Directions:
1. Heat olive oil in a pan over medium. Add onion and cook until translucent, about 5 minutes.
2. Lower heat and add quinoa, stirring for about 2 minutes to toast.
3. Stir in water, bouillon, pepper, and thyme. Raise heat to high and bring to a boil. Cover, reduce heat to low, and simmer for about 5 minutes.
4. Stir in the carrot. Cover and simmer until all water is absorbed—this should take about 10 minutes.
5. Turn heat off and add tomatoes and spinach. Stir until spinach is wilted, about 2 minutes.
6. Serve hot as a main or side dish.

Nutritional Information (Per Serving)
Calories: 196
Fat: 5.1 g
Sat Fat: 0.7 g
Carbohydrates: 31.6 g

Fiber: 4.3 g
Sugar: 2 g
Protein: 6.8 g
Sodium: 67 mg

Dinner is usually the main event when it comes to meal planning. This doesn't have to change when you're managing diabetes and trying to keep your blood sugar regulated. When you're putting your dinner plans together, keep in mind what you've already eaten during the day. If you've had a lot of fiber and whole grain carbohydrates, it's a good time to focus mostly on vegetables and lean protein. Conversely, if you've managed to avoid carbs during your other meals and snacks, dinner is a good time to have some pasta, rice, or any other of your favorite foods that will keep you satisfied and happy.

Conclusion

To manage your diabetes and prevent dangerous complications, it is necessary to learn what to eat, how much to eat, when to eat, and why you shouldn't eat some types of food. It is easy to mismanage diabetes, as unhealthy junk foods and processed foods can be found everywhere, but if you really want to control your diabetes instead of it controlling you, you need to adopt a healthy diet. It's best to consult a dietitian or a doctor to get a recommendation that's suited to your specific condition.

I hope the diabetic recipes in this book have given you some new ideas for preparing delicious and healthy homemade meals. Regular exercise, taking your medication on time, eating low carb, low sodium, and low fat meals—all of these combined will help you to lose weight and keep your blood sugar levels within your target range.

Finally, I want to thank you for reading my book. If you enjoyed the book, please take the time to share your thoughts and post a review on the Diabetic Recipes: Healthy and Delicious Low-Carb Recipes to Lower Blood Sugar Amazon book page. It would be greatly appreciated!

Best wishes,
Savannah Gibbs

Check Out My Other Books

Instant Pot Cookbook for Two: Easy, Delicious and Healthy Instant Pot Recipes for Two
https://www.amazon.com/Instant-Pot-Cookbook-Two-Delicious-ebook/dp/B0795V4HLH/

Crock Pot Cookbook: Easy, Delicious, and Healthy Crock Pot Recipes for Busy People
https://www.amazon.com/dp/B077P11VKQ/

Spiralizer Cookbook: Easy, Delicious, and Healthy Recipes
for Your Spiralizer
https://www.amazon.com/Spiralizer-Cookbook-Delicious-Healthy-Recipes-ebook/dp/B074RHBNM7/

Fermentation for Beginners: Delicious Fermented Vegetable
Recipes for Better Digestion and Health
https://www.amazon.com/Fermentation-Beginners-Delicious-Fermented-Vegetable-ebook/dp/B0754RLGVC/

Mediterranean Diet Cookbook: Easy and Delicious
Mediterranean Diet Recipes to Lose Weight and Lower Your
Risk of Heart Disease
https://www.amazon.com/dp/B071RMNKJG/

Clean Eating Cookbook: Quick and Easy Clean Eating
Recipes to Lose Weight and Live Healthy
https://www.amazon.com/dp/B06XX7R39Y/

Weight Loss Smoothies: 45 Delicious Smoothie Recipes to
Lose Weight and Get Healthy
https://www.amazon.com/Weight-Loss-Smoothies-Delicious-Smoothie-ebook/dp/B06XHF9RXM/

Electric Pressure Cooker Cookbook: Quick, Easy, and Healthy Electric Pressure Cooker Recipes for Your Family
https://www.amazon.com/Electric-Pressure-Cooker-Cookbook-Healthy-ebook/dp/B06XD7RRHZ/